instei

32
Wok Dishes

by Norman Weinstein

BARRON'S

Woodbury, New York • London • Toronto • Sydney

All inquiries should be addressed to:

Barron's Educational Series, Inc.
113 Crossways Park Drive
Woodbury, New York 11797

International Standard Book
No. 0-8120-5532-2
Library of Congress Catalog Card
No. 83-6431

**Library of Congress Cataloging
in Publication Data**
Weinstein, Norman, 1938-
    32 wok dishes.

    (Barron's easy cooking series)
    Includes index.
    1. Wok cookery.   2. Cookery,
Chinese.   I. Title.
II. Title: Thirty-two wok dishes.   III. Series.
TX724.5.C5W38   1983   641.7'7   83-6431
ISBN 0-8120-5532-2

PRINTED IN THE
UNITED STATES OF AMERICA
3 4 5 6   9 8 7 6 5 4 3 2 1

Credits

Photography
Color photographs: Irwin Horowitz
Food preparation: Andrea Swenson
Stylist: Hal Walter

Author Norman Weinstein is the founder of
    The Hot Wok, a cooking school and
    catering business in Brooklyn, New York.
    He is on the staff of the New York
    Cooking Center, and has demonstrated his
    wok-cooking skills at Macy's and on various
    television shows.

Cover and book design Milton Glaser, Inc.

Series editor Carole Berglie

e Chinese kitchen requires fewer tools at less
st than most major cuisines. The ancient ves-
l—the wok—serves many functions and there-
re replaces many Western utensils. To prepare
e recipes in this book, you will need 2 woks—
e for oil cooking and one for water-steaming. In
dition, you will need a domed cover for the
ok, a large strainer for removing food from the
ok, 1 or 2 Chinese-style spatulas, a 12-inch alu-
num steaming rack or bamboo steamer set, a
arp cleaver or chef's knife, a paring knife, and an
ortment of bowls and platters.

BOUT YOUR WOK

ur wok should be 14 inches in diameter and be
de of rolled carbon steel. It should have a flat-
ned bottom (the smaller the better) to adapt to
e American stove, especially the electric stove.
season your new wok, scour thoroughly to re-
ve any oil coating. Dry thoroughly and place
er medium heat. Add 2 tablespoons of cooking
 and rub into the wok with a wad of paper tow-
. Discard the towels as they become gritty.
hen the wok seems dry, turn off the heat, let
e wok cool, then rinse with hot water; paper-
wel dry, place back on the stove, and repeat the
ole process. The wok will begin to darken and
e towels will no longer pick up grit. Let the wok
ol, wash with hot water only (no soap), dry
oroughly, place on the stove, and heat until va-
rs appear. Follow these final washing, drying, and
ating instructions after every use.
 The steaming wok needs no seasoning but
ould be initially scoured, then washed, dried, and
ated after every use to prevent rusting.

WOK TECHNIQUES

There are some basic techniques, easy to learn:

● **Stir-frying**   Stir-frying involves cooking pre-
cut pieces of food in small amounts of oil over *high
heat* for short periods of time. The wok must be
pre-heated until vapors appear before any oil is
added. The oil must be heated before any food is
added. The food must be swirled constantly in the
hot oil to assure evenness of cooking. Your mari-
nated and coated meats will not stick to the wok
if these rules are adhered to. Avoid the common
error of adding too much food to the wok at one
time. This reduces available heat and can seriously
mar the outcome of your recipe. Follow the instructions to cook the food (especially meats) in
batches.

● **Deep-frying**   This technique involves the use
of considerably more oil than stir-frying but this
oil, rather than the hot surface of the wok, acts as
the heat-transfer medium. The oil should be
heated to approximately 375 degrees before the
food is added. Shrimp shells become crisp and edible, a surprising contrast to the succulent meat.
Batters seal and become crunchy at this temperature. Deep-fried steak pieces are crisp on the outside while still moist and tender on the inside. As
with stir-frying, care must be taken not to lower
the oil temperature by adding too much food at
one time. Deep-fry oil can often be re-used if fil-
tered into a clean heat-proof bowl, allowed to
cool, then stored in a covered jar in the refrigera-
tor or cool place.

● **Steaming**   In this method of cooking, the wok
is used as a water vessel in which either a perfo-
rated aluminum tray or a bamboo basket is placed.

The food platter is set atop the tray or basket, covered, and steamed•over *high heat*. Do not interchange your oil and water woks otherwise your oil wok will need re-seasoning.

GENERAL HINTS ON PREPARING THE RECIPES

● **Cooking times**   Consider all time indications as approximate. Available heat, the quantity of food added, and the size of your pieces will determine when to remove or add ingredients. Use your judgment. Err on the side of underdone. If necessary, test a morsel, preferably the largest one. (Try, however, to cut like ingredients the same size.)

● **Quantity and type of oil**   The amount of oil needed to stir-fry or deep-fry will vary according to the shape of the wok used; the larger the flat area, the more oil needed. Oil quantities given are, therefore, approximate. For stir-frying especially, have more oil available than the recipe calls for. Peanut or corn oil are preferred.

● **Cornstarch**   Use a light dusting when marinating meats—just enough to barely coat the top surface. For thickening a sauce, use a mixture of cornstarch and liquid the consistency of milk. Add it slowly and stir constantly while adding.

● **Ginger**   If you are fortunate, fresh gingerroot is available to you. Buy as large a piece as you can find. Peel it and store in a container of dry sherry wine. Break off whatever size knob is indicated, cut what is needed, put the remainder back in the wine. Refrigerated, it will last quite a while. The flavored wine may be used where wine is indicated in the recipe. Replenish as needed.

● **Organization**   Preparation and organization are essential to the fast pace of Chinese cooking. Much of the preparation can be done hours in advance and refrigerated until ready for use. If possible, allow yourself a few hours to relax between preparation and cooking. Before beginning to cook, have all ingredients and utensils at hand. Line up ingredients in the order they will be used, from beginning oil to final cornstarch mixture or garnish.

COOKING RICE

Chinese food is traditionally served with rice. Here is my favorite recipe: Place 2 cups of rice in a 2½ quart saucepan. Add water 1 inch above the rice. Bring to the boil, cover, and reduce to the barest simmer. Cook for 25 minutes. Remove from the heat and let stand for 20 minutes. Fluff gently with a fork and serve in individual bowls as is the custom.

ABOUT THE RECIPES

In order to make this book useful to the largest number of people, every effort has been made to use obtainable ingredients while retaining the spirit of Chinese cooking. All recipes in this book serve from **4 to 6 persons,** depending on whether you are making the dish as a main course or are serving it with other dishes, as would be done for an oriental meal. Here, then, are 32 Wok Dishes; some classic and ageless, some modern, some whimsical. They cover a wide range of flavors: salty, sweet, sour, bland, and hot, and were chosen or created to demonstrate the amazing versatility of one of the world's great cuisines.

OUT THE RECIPE ANALYSES

each recipe in this book, you'll note that we
e provided data on the quantities of protein,
sodium, carbohydrates, and potassium, as well
he number of calories (kcal) per serving. If you
on a low-calorie diet or are watching your in-
e of sodium, for example, these figures should
p you gauge your eating habits and help you
nce your meals. Bear in mind, however, that
calculations are fundamentally estimates, and
to be followed only in a very general way. The
ual quantity of fat, for example, that may be
tained in a given portion will vary with the
lity of meat you buy or with how much care
take in draining off fat. Likewise, all the figures
vary somewhat depending on how large the
tions are that you serve. These analyses are
ed on the number of portions given for each
ipe. Since each recipe in this book serves from
o 6 persons, based on whether you are using
recipe as a main dish or serving it with accom-
ying dishes, we have chosen arbitrarily to give
portion breakdowns as for **4 persons.**
here are other differences too, which make
data helpful but only with an understanding of
ir limitations. There are variations in the quan-
that would constitute an edible portion of
at, for example, and there are varying sodium
els found in different brands of different prod-
s. To add to all this, the information on oriental
ducts is not always available or is incomplete,
we had to make some estimates. We advise
to use this data, but if you must follow a rigid
t, then we suggest you consult your doctor.

MAIL-ORDER SOURCES

If you are fortunate enough to live in a city where
there are oriental markets, than you can obtain
everything you need to make the recipes in this
book. We avoided including esoteric ingredients,
and most everything should be available in your lo-
cal supermarket. In the event you wish to obtain
dried and canned ingredients or Chinese equip-
ment through reliable mail-order houses, the fol-
lowing are suggested:

Anzen Japanese Foods
736 NE Union Avenue
Portland, Oregon 97232

Woks 'N Things
2234 South Wentworth
    Avenue
Chicago, Illinois 60616

Queen's Fresh Produce
5714 Locke Avenue
Fort Worth, Texas 76116

The Dragon Trading
    Company
943 Dopler
Akron, Ohio 44303

The Red Road Market
4016 Red Road
Miami, Florida 33155

East Asia Market
1806 Polk Street
Houston, Texas 77003

The Oriental Market
502 Pampas Street
Austin, Texas 78752

Jungs Oriental Food
2519 North Fitzhugh
Dallas, Texas 75204

Friendship Enterprises
3415 Payne Avenue
Cleveland, Ohio 44114

Hall One Company
3126 St. Clair Avenue
Cleveland, Ohio 44114

IELD

to 6 servings
r serving (4)
ories 179, protein 8 g,
12 g, sodium 607 mg,
bohydrates 13 g,
assium 759 mg

IME

to 15 minutes
preparation
to 4 minutes cooking

INGREDIENTS

1 large bunch broccoli
1 knob gingerroot, 2 inches long
2 cloves garlic
3 tablespoons oil

SAUCE

3 tablespoons oyster sauce
2 tablespoons chicken broth
2 teaspoons dry sherry

Separate broccoli flowerets from the main stalk, leaving 1½ inches of stem. Trim the tough outer skin from the stem, ① then trim the stem to a point. Peel the ginger and cut into 6 to 8 thin slices across the grain ②. Peel and slice the garlic. Combine the sauce ingredients.

Heat a wok. Add the oil and heat for 10 seconds. Add the ginger and garlic and stir for 10 seconds, then add the broccoli. Stir to coat thoroughly with oil, continuing until the color begins to change toward a darker green ③. Add the sauce down the side, stir to coat. Cover the wok and cook for 1 minute. Remove to a platter and serve immediately.

VARIATIONS Add 1 cup cubed, pressed bean curd along with the sauce and proceed as above but call the dish Jade and Ivory. Add 1 or 2 scallions cut into 2-inch pieces along with the ginger and garlic.

NOTE Reserve the broccoli stalks for another dish. See Recipe 5 for a suggested use. See Recipe 17 for directions on pressing bean curd.

ELD

to 6 servings

r serving (4)

ries 504 g, protein 27 g,
36 g, sodium 1639 mg,
bohydrates 20 g,
assium 323 mg

ME

minutes preparation
hours pressing
minutes cooking

INGREDIENTS

6–8 large chicken wings
4 squares firm bean curd
4 knobs gingerroot, about 1 inch long
6 scallions
4 tablespoons black soy sauce
3 tablespoons dry sherry
5–6 tablespoons oil
2–3 tablespoons brownulated sugar
¾–1 cup chicken broth
2 tablespoons cornstarch mixed with
   ¼ cup cold water

Have your butcher cut the wings into 6 pieces, cutting across the bones. Press the bean curd until fairly firm (see Recipe 17). Smash the ginger ①. Wash and trim the scallions. Separate scallion greens from root end then cut into 1-inch pieces ②; lightly smash the root ends. Combine the soy sauce and sherry. When bean curd is ready, cut into 9 uniform pieces.

Heat a wok. Add 2 to 3 tablespoons oil and heat for 15 seconds. Add 2 pieces of ginger and half the smashed scallions; stir for 15 seconds. Add half the chicken pieces and stir over high heat until the wings begin to brown. Remove contents with a strainer to a work platter ③. Add more oil if necessary, heat, and then add the remaining ginger and smashed scallions. Brown the remaining wing pieces.

Return the first batch of chicken, ginger, and scallions to the wok, pour the soy-wine mixture down the sides, and stir to coat. Add the sugar and enough broth to come to within an inch of the surface. Stir, bring to the boil, reduce to a simmer, cover, and cook 15 minutes. Remove the cover, add the bean curd and scallion greens, and simmer another 10 minutes.

Restir the cornstarch and water mixture. Return heat to high, slowly add the cornstarch and thicken the sauce to the consistency of honey. Serve immediately or place in a heavy casserole and keep warm until needed.

NOTE *Large roasting chicken wings are excellent for this dish. The bean curd can be prepared days in advance; store covered in cold water and change water daily. If obtainable, use a 1½-inch chunk of rock sugar in place of the brownulated sugar—it will give the sauce a nice glaze.*

3

ELD

‚ 6 servings

serving (4)

ies 601, protein 36 g,
‚3 g, sodium 1015 mg,
hydrates 22 g,
ssium 486 mg

ME

to 15 minutes
oreparation
minutes chilling
‚ 10 minutes cooking

INGREDIENTS

1 pound boneless chicken breast
2 small or 1 large red bell pepper(s)
4 scallions
6 knobs gingerroot, 1 inch long
6 cloves garlic
1½ tablespoons dry sherry
1 tablespoon thin soy sauce
¼ teaspoon sugar
1 egg white

Cornstarch to coat
½ cup oil
¾ cup dry-roasted unsalted peanuts

SAUCE

¼ cup hoisin sauce
1½ tablespoons Red Devil sauce
1 tablespoon Worcestershire sauce

Trim the chicken breast of fat. Wrap the chicken in aluminum foil, and chill until firm but not frozen.

Cut the pepper(s) and scallions into ½-inch dice ①. Smash the ginger and the garlic. Combine the sauce ingredients; cover everything until ready for use.

Remove fillet from chicken ② and cut meat into ½-inch strips ③ then ½-inch dice. Place in a bowl and add the sherry, soy sauce, and sugar. Mix well; add the egg white and mix again; sprinkle cornstarch on top and mix again. Refrigerate for at least 30 minutes or until ready to use. Bring to room temperature, coat with 1 tablespoon oil before stir-frying.

Heat a wok and add 1 tablespoon oil. Heat for 30 seconds, then add the peppers and stir for 30 seconds. Add the scallions and stir for another 30 seconds. Remove to the work platter.

Add the remaining oil to the wok. Heat for 1 minute, then add the ginger and, when lightly browned, add the garlic. Remove and discard both when the garlic browns.

Stir-fry the chicken pieces in the flavored oil in 3 batches for 30 to 40 seconds each, but allow the oil to reheat between each batch. Remove the chicken to the work platter with a strainer.

Add more oil to the wok if necessary. When hot, add the sauce and bring to the bubble, stirring all the while. Add the contents of the work platter and the peanuts. Mix well to coat with the sauce. Place on a serving platter and serve.

4

IELD

to 6 servings
r serving (4)
ories 142, protein 14 g,
8 g, sodium 1115 mg,
rbohydrates 4 g,
tassium 262 mg

IME

to 10 minutes
preparation
minutes resting
minutes cooking

INGREDIENTS

1 fish, salt or fresh water (sea bass,
   snapper, yellow pike, salmon, trout,
   etc.), about 1½–2 pounds and no
   longer than 12 inches
3 tablespoons dry sherry
3 scallion stalks
3 thin slices gingerroot, about 2½ by
   1 inches
3 tablespoons thin soy sauce
2 tablespoons oriental sesame oil

Have the fish cleaned and scaled but leave the head and tail on. (If any cutting has to be done, trim the tail.) Holding your knife at a 45-degree angle, slash the fish to the center bone at 1½-inch intervals ①. Place the fish on a platter, sprinkle with the sherry, and let stand 20 minutes.

Trim and wash the scallions, slit in half lengthwise, and cut into 2-inch pieces. Shred the ginger slices into matchstick pieces ②. Sprinkle the soy sauce and sesame oil atop the fish, then crisscross the ginger shreds on top of the fish and place the scallion pieces atop the ginger.

Place the steaming rack inside the steaming wok ③. Add 5 to 6 cups of water to the wok and bring to the boil. Lower the platter onto the rack, cover the wok, and steam the fish over high heat for 12 to 15 minutes, depending on the size and girth. The fish is done when the flesh pulls away from the bone easily.

Remove the platter from the wok with a plate lifter or pot holders. Place the fish platter on a larger platter and bring to the table. The fish is eaten by removing the sections from the bone, working from tail to head. When the top side of the fish has been devoured, lift up the center bone and finish the meat underneath. Don't forget the meat behind the head, and be sure to give the guest of honor the cheek pieces.

VARIATION Rinse 2 tablespoons of salted black beans in hot water to remove excess salt, then sprinkle over the fish.

INGREDIENTS

1-pound strip flank steak
2 teaspoons thin soy sauce
2 teaspoons dry sherry
1 egg white
Cornstarch to coat
Oil for stir-frying
1 bunch broccoli
salt
2 tablespoons salted black beans
2 cloves garlic
1 teaspoon dry sherry

2 tablespoons cornstarch
1 cup sliced bamboo shoots

SAUCE

¾ cup chicken broth
1 tablespoon black soy sauce
2 tablespoons oyster sauce
2 teaspoons dry sherry
2 teaspoons sugar

ELD

6 servings
serving (4)
ries 501, protein 33 g,
1 g, sodium 1216 mg,
ohydrates 25 g,
ssium 996 mg

ME

10 minutes
preparation
minutes chilling
10 minutes cooking

Chill the steak until firm but not frozen. Cut on the bias into very thin slices about 2 inches by 1 inch ①. Place in a bowl and add the soy sauce and sherry. Mix well, add the egg white, and mix again. Dust with cornstarch ②. Mix and refrigerate at least 30 minutes. Bring to room temperature before cooking, and coat with oil.

Separate the flowerets from the broccoli stalk. Break the flowerets into uniform pieces, then remove the tough outer skin from the stalk with a paring knife ③. Cut the stalk on the bias into ⅛-inch slices.

Place a colander in the sink. Bring 10 cups of water to the boil, add a pinch of salt, then add the broccoli. Remove broccoli to the colander when it turns dark green (no longer than 15 seconds). Rinse with cold water immediately to stop the cooking, and pat or spin dry. Reserve for later.

Rinse the black beans under hot water. Peel and mince the garlic. Combine with the beans and moisten with the sherry. Combine the sauce ingredients. Remove 5 tablespoons of sauce and combine with the cornstarch. Do this just before beginning to cook.

Heat a wok. Add 4 tablespoons oil. Swirl about for 30 seconds, then stir-fry the beef in 3 batches, for 30 to 45 seconds each batch and adding more oil as necessary, allowing it to re-heat before adding meat. Using a strainer, remove the beef to a platter. Add more oil if necessary, heat, then add the beans and garlic. Stir for 15 seconds, then add the broccoli and bamboo shoots. Stir for 30 seconds. Remove to the platter.

Add 1 tablespoon oil, heat, and add the sauce. Bring to the boil, gradually add the cornstarch mixture stirring constantly, and thicken to the consistency of honey. Add the beef and vegetables, stir to coat with sauce, and serve.

YIELD

to 6 servings

r serving (4)
ries 443, protein 20 g,
35 g, sodium 804 mg,
bohydrates 13 g,
assium 532 mg

TIME

to 15 minutes
preparation
minutes chilling
to 12 minutes cooking

INGREDIENTS

4–5 chicken thighs
I teaspoon salt
I tablespoon dry sherry
I egg white
Cornstarch to coat
I tablespoon oil
I pound thin-stalked asparagus
3 cloves garlic
¾ cup chicken broth
I tablespoon dry sherry
I tablespoon cornstarch

3 tablespoons cold water
6–8 tablespoons oil for stir-frying
4–5 chunks gingerroot, about I inch
    thick
I teaspoon oriental sesame oil

Remove the chicken meat from the bones ①. Trim the fat. Cut meat into uniform bite-sized pieces and place in a bowl. Add ½ teaspoon salt and the sherry. Mix well, then add the egg white. Mix again. Dust with cornstarch, and mix again. Refrigerate for at least 30 minutes. Bring to room temperature before cooking. If stuck together, coat with the I tablespoon oil to separate.

Snap off the tough ends of the asparagus. Cut the stalk on the bias into 1½-inch pieces, giving a quarter turn after each cut ②. Smash the ginger, peel the garlic and cut into thin slices. Combine the broth and sherry. Just before cooking, combine the cornstarch and water.

Heat a wok. Add 3 to 4 tablespoons oil. Heat for 30 seconds, then stir-fry the chicken ③ in 3 batches for 1½ to 2 minutes each, reheating the wok after each batch and adding more oil as necessary. Remove the chicken to a work platter with a strainer.

Add I to 2 tablespoons oil to the wok. Over high heat, lightly brown the ginger. Reduce the heat and add the garlic slices. Stir for 30 seconds, then add the remaining salt. Stir to mix well. Add the asparagus, then turn up the heat and stir for I minute. With a strainer, remove the contents of the wok to the platter.

Add the broth mixture to the wok and bring to the boil. Gradually add the cornstarch mixture, stirring constantly. When the consistency of honey is attained, add the chicken and asparagus. Stir to coat with sauce, then add the sesame oil. Mix and remove to a serving platter. Serve immediately.

VARIATION Cut 3 or 4 scallions to the size of the asparagus. Add after the ginger, and proceed with the recipe. Add a red bell pepper cut into 1-inch squares along with the asparagus.

ELD

6 servings
serving (4)
ies 604, protein 32 g,
8 g, sodium 361 mg,
ohydrates 8 g,
ssium 517 mg

ME

to 15 minutes
preparation
minutes chilling
to 12 minutes cooking

INGREDIENTS

1 1/4 pounds boneless shell steak
    (New York cut)
Cornstarch to coat
2 bunches watercress
1/2 cup oil
1 thin slice gingerroot
12 large shrimp in the shell

SAUCE

2 tablespoons tomato catsup
2 teaspoons Worcestershire sauce
1/2 teaspoon sugar
1 teaspoon black soy sauce
2 tablespoons chicken broth
1 teaspoon oriental sesame oil
Freshly ground black pepper

Remove fat and tail piece (if left on) from steak. Cut steak in half lengthwise, then cut each half on the bias into 8 pieces ①. Place in a bowl, add the cornstarch, and work the starch into the meat with the fingers. Refrigerate at least 30 minutes. Bring to room temperature before cooking.

Wash the watercress and pat dry. Place a heatproof bowl near the stove before starting to cook. Combine the sauce ingredients.

Heat a wok. Add the oil. Heat for at least 1 minute, then toss in the ginger. If it sizzles immediately, remove and add half the steak pieces. Stir and turn to coat with oil. Remove when the pieces begin to crust lightly ②. Allow oil to heat for 10 seconds, then put the pieces back in. Remove immediately to the work platter and cook remaining steak the same way.

Allow the oil to reheat for 10 seconds. Add the shrimp and stir and turn constantly. Remove when the shells are pink-orange and the meat at the top is solid white ③. Drain oil into the bowl, leaving a thin slick in the wok. Reheat wok and add the cress; stir until wilted but not soggy. Remove and place around the perimeter of the serving platter.

Spoon 1 tablespoon of the oil into the wok. Coat the bottom, add the sauce. Bring sauce to the bubble, then add steak and shrimp. Stir to coat with sauce, then place in center of serving platter. Serve immediately.

NOTE The rareness of the steak can be controlled by the thickness of the cut, the intensity of the heat, and the cooking time. Experiment to your preference.

SERVING VARIATION Place the watercress in the center of a warm serving platter. Separate steak and shrimp and place at opposite ends.

8

*ELD

o 6 servings

r serving (4)
ries 490, protein 35 g,
27 g, sodium 1298 mg,
bohydrates 30 g,
assium 717 mg

*ME

minutes preparation
minutes chilling
o 10 minutes cooking

INGREDIENTS

2 boned chicken breasts, 1 to 1 1/4
  pounds
1 teaspoon thin soy sauce
1 teaspoon dry sherry
1 egg white
Cornstarch to coat
Peel of 1 medium thin-skinned orange
3 scallions
6 tablespoons oil

1 bunch broccoli (flowerets only)
6 dried chili peppers
6 slices gingerroot, about 1/4 inch thick

SAUCE

3 tablespoons dry sherry
3 tablespoons thin soy sauce
3 tablespoons red wine vinegar
1 1/2 tablespoons sugar
1 1/2 tablespoons orange juice

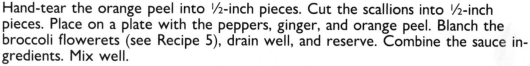

Trim the fat and gristle from the breasts and separate from the inner fillet ①. Cut the breasts lengthwise into 3 sections ②. Cut all sections on the bias into 1 1/2-inch pieces ③. Place in a bowl and add the soy sauce and wine. Mix well. Add the egg white; mix again. Dust with cornstarch. Mix well and refrigerate at least 30 minutes. Bring to room temperature and coat with oil before cooking.

Hand-tear the orange peel into 1/2-inch pieces. Cut the scallions into 1/2-inch pieces. Place on a plate with the peppers, ginger, and orange peel. Blanch the broccoli flowerets (see Recipe 5), drain well, and reserve. Combine the sauce ingredients. Mix well.

Heat a wok and add 1/4 cup oil. Heat for 1 minute or until white smoke appears, then stir-fry the chicken pieces in 3 batches for 45 seconds each batch. Allow the oil to reheat between batches and remove the chicken to your work platter with a strainer.

Add the remaining 2 tablespoons oil. Heat for 30 seconds, then add the peppers. Stir until lightly charred. Add the ginger slices, and stir 1 minute. Remove and discard both. Add the orange peel, stir for 1 minute, then add the scallions and stir for 30 seconds.

Mix the sauce and pour around the sides of the wok. Bring to the boil, add the chicken, then add the broccoli. Stir to mix well. Remove to a platter and serve immediately.

VARIATION *Thicken the sauce slightly by adding a mixture of 2 teaspoons cornstarch and 3 tablespoons sauce mixture; add to wok slowly, stirring constantly, when the sauce comes to the boil.*

ELD

6 servings

serving (4)
ies 521, protein 24 g,
2 g, sodium 804 mg,
hydrates 15 g,
ssium 553 mg

ME

o 15 minutes
reparation
o 18 minutes cooking

INGREDIENTS

1 pound boneless pork loin
1 tablespoon thin soy sauce
1 tablespoon dry sherry
Cornstarch to coat
2 stalks celery
1 large green pepper
½ small zucchini
1½ cups oil
1 cup walnut halves

SAUCE

3 tablespoons chicken broth
1 tablespoon black soy sauce
2 teaspoons red wine vinegar
2 teaspoons sugar
¼ teaspoon Tabasco
1 teaspoon cornstarch

Trim the pork of top fat. Cut into ⅜-inch slices, then into sticks, then into dice ①. Place in a bowl and add soy sauce and sherry. Mix well. Dust with cornstarch and mix again. Reserve.

Trim and string the celery ②. Dice celery, pepper, and zucchini to the size of the pork. Mix sauce ingredients and set aside.

Add the oil to the wok and heat to 375 degrees. Fry the walnuts until deep golden ③. Remove with a strainer to a work platter and drain oil to a waiting heatproof bowl.

Place wok back on stove, heat and add 3 tablespoons of the deep-fry oil. Heat for 10 seconds and add half the pork, stir to coat with oil, and separate. Remove to the work platter when it begins to brown and stir-fry the remaining pork. Remove and combine on platter with first batch.

Add more oil if necessary, heat for 10 seconds, then add celery. Stir 20 seconds, add peppers, and stir 20 seconds. Add zucchini and stir another 20 seconds. Return the pork and walnuts to the wok, swirl the sauce down the sides of the wok, and stir to mix well. Remove to a platter and serve immediately.

ELD

6 servings

serving (4)
ies 362, protein 27 g,
0 g, sodium 873 mg,
hydrates 15 g,
ssium 780 mg

ME

10 minutes
reparation
to 20 minutes cooking

INGREDIENTS

1 pound firm-fleshed fish fillets
1/2 teaspoon salt
Pinch of sugar
1 egg white
Cornstarch to coat
3 stalks bok choy with leaves
1 can (10 ounces) straw mushrooms,
    drained
12 snow peas
4 waterchestnuts
3 cloves garlic
Dry sherry

6 cups oil
1 egg white, beaten
2 teaspoons sesame oil

SAUCE

1 cup chicken broth
1 tablespoon gin
2 tablespoons sweet vermouth
1/2 teaspoon salt (if necessary)
Freshly ground pepper
2 tablespoons cornstarch

Cut the fillets in half lengthwise, then on the bias into 1¼-inch pieces (1). Place in a bowl. Add salt and sugar and mix gently with fingers. Lightly beat the egg white, add to bowl, and mix gently. Coat fish with cornstarch; mix and reserve.

Split bok choy down the middle. Cut on the bias into 1-inch pieces (2); include some leaf for color. Trim the snow peas. Cut waterchestnuts into thin slices. Peel and slice garlic; moisten with dry sherry.

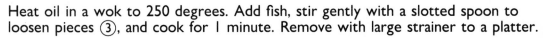

Combine broth, gin, wine, salt, and pepper for sauce. Remove ¼ cup and mix with the 2 tablespoons of cornstarch.

Heat oil in a wok to 250 degrees. Add fish, stir gently with a slotted spoon to loosen pieces (3), and cook for 1 minute. Remove with large strainer to a platter.

Strain the oil into a heatproof bowl. Reheat wok and add 3 tablespoons of the oil. Reduce heat and add garlic. Stir 30 seconds, turn up heat, and add vegetables. Stir for 30 seconds, then remove to platter.

Add the sauce to wok. Bring to a boil, then thicken to the desired consistency with the cornstarch mixture, adding slowly and stirring continuously. Reduce heat source, pour beaten egg white on top. Let set for 10 seconds. Fold slowly until soft white threads appear. Add fish, vegetables, and sesame oil and stir to mix. Place on serving platter and serve immediately.

VARIATION Substitute sliced fresh mushrooms for the straw mushrooms; add with the garlic.

YIELD

to 6 servings
serving (4)
ries 251, protein 16 g,
14 g, sodium 1327 mg,
ohydrates 14 g,
ssium 264 mg

TIME

minutes preparation
our chilling
to 18 minutes cooking

INGREDIENTS

1 pound large shrimp
¼ cup coarse salt
1 egg white, beaten
Cornstarch to coat
4 cloves garlic
2 scallions
6 thin slices peeled gingerroot, about
   2½ by 1 inches
¼ cup red wine vinegar
2 tablespoons thin soy sauce

2 tablespoons sugar or to taste
4 cups oil
1 large juice orange for garnish

Peel shrimp. Make a deep incision along their backs ①, then remove and discard the vein. Place shrimp in a bowl and add one-third the salt. Whip with a wooden spoon until a white foam appears on the sides of the bowl ②. Rinse the shrimp thoroughly with cold water, and repeat this whole process 2 more times. Pat the shrimp dry, mix with the beaten egg white, and coat with 2 or 3 tablespoons of cornstarch. Mix well, then refrigerate for at least 1 hour.

Mince the garlic and ginger. Slit the scallions into quarters, then mince; combine with garlic and ginger. In a separate dish, combine the vinegar, soy sauce, and sugar.

Add oil to the wok and begin heating to 350 degrees. Set a colander over a large heatproof bowl and have nearby.

Lower the shrimp into the hot oil ③. Stir to separate, and cook for about 2 minutes until no longer translucent. Pour the shrimp and oil into the colander.

Add 3 tablespoons of the oil to the wok. Heat for 15 seconds, then add the minced ingredients. Stir for 30 seconds, then add the vinegar mixture. Bring to the boil, add the shrimp, and stir to coat for 15 seconds. Remove to a platter garnished with half-moon slices of orange.

NOTE *The sugar quantity will vary according to the acidic strength of the vinegar used. The salt-whipping process described above removes starch from the shrimp and renders them more crunchy.*

6 servings

serving (4)

es 90, protein 3 g,
g, sodium 133 mg,
hydrates 5 g,
sium 496 mg

20 minutes
reparation
3 minutes cooking

INGREDIENTS

6 cups stemmed spinach leaves
12–16 fresh mushrooms
2 cloves garlic
2 tablespoons oil
⅛ teaspoon salt
Fresh black pepper

Rinse the spinach in the sink or a large bowl filled with cold water to remove sand ①. Pat or spin dry. Wipe mushrooms with a damp towel. Cut off stem ends but do not de-stem; cut into ¼-inch slices to yield 2 cups. Peel and slice garlic ②.

Heat a wok. Add the oil, heat 5 seconds, then add the garlic. Stir 10 seconds, then add the mushrooms and toss to coat with oil. Stir 10 seconds, then add the spinach. Press down with the spatula ③. Stir constantly, bringing the contents from the bottom to the top, coating the spinach with hot oil. Cook until the spinach has wilted but is not yet soggy. Sprinkle with the salt and pepper to taste. Mix well, then remove to a platter and serve immediately.

ELD

o 6 servings

serving (4)
ries 456, protein 23 g,
l7 g, sodium 812 mg,
ohydrates 53 g,
ssium 771 mg

ME

minutes preparation
o 7 minutes cooking

INGREDIENTS

I cup shredded, leftover steak
I small red bell pepper
I small green bell pepper
4 medium leaves Chinese cabbage
3 scallions
2 cloves garlic
4 cups spinach
½ pound vermicelli
3–4 tablespoons oil for stir-frying

SAUCE

3 tablespoons chicken broth
I tablespoon black soy sauce
2 tablespoons oyster sauce
I tablespoon oriental sesame oil
⅛ teaspoon freshly ground black or
    white pepper
½ teaspoon sugar

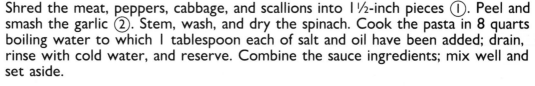

Shred the meat, peppers, cabbage, and scallions into 1½-inch pieces ①. Peel and smash the garlic ②. Stem, wash, and dry the spinach. Cook the pasta in 8 quarts boiling water to which I tablespoon each of salt and oil have been added; drain, rinse with cold water, and reserve. Combine the sauce ingredients; mix well and set aside.

Heat a wok and add the oil. Heat for 15 seconds, then add the shredded meat. Stir for 15 seconds and add the peppers. Stir 30 seconds, then move the ingredients aside and add the garlic. Stir the garlic in the pool of oil, then add the cabbage and scallions. Stir to mix well, then add the pasta. Mix the ingredients, then pour in the sauce down the sides of the wok ③. Add the spinach and keep mixing to thoroughly coat the noodles with sauce. When the spinach leaves have wilted (don't let them become soggy), remove the contents of the wok to a serving platter. Serve immediately.

NOTE As with fried rice, lo mein (tossed noodles), is the perfect vehicle for leftovers. The only requirement is that everything (except the spinach) be shredded to conform with the shape of the noodles.

?ELD

6 servings

serving (4)
ies 409, protein 20 g,
0 g, sodium 366 mg,
ohydrates 14 g,
ssium 513 mg

?ME

to 15 minutes
?reparation
6 minutes cooking

INGREDIENTS

¾ pound ground sirloin
2 egg whites
1 tablespoon cornstarch
2–3 thin fresh red chilies
10 waterchestnuts
1 head iceberg lettuce
2 tablespoons oil
1 cup freshly cooked or frozen green
    peas

SAUCE

2 tablespoons chicken broth
2 teaspoons thin soy sauce
Freshly ground pepper to taste
1 tablespoon oriental sesame oil
1 teaspoon cornstarch

Mix the beef thoroughly with the egg whites ① and cornstarch. Cut the chilies crosswise into ⅛-inch pieces; cut the waterchestnuts into eighths ②. Combine the sauce ingredients. Select 8 large, well-rounded lettuce leaves. Place on a large platter.

Heat a wok. Add the oil and heat for 15 seconds, then add the chilies. Stir 10 seconds, and add the waterchestnuts. Stir 10 seconds; add the beef and stir vigorously to separate the grains. Cook until the beef has completely lost its raw color and the grains are well defined.

Move the beef to the side of the wok. Add the sauce to the vacated space and stir to thicken with the edge of the spatula ③. Mix well, then add the peas; stir to mix once more. Remove to a bowl, then bring bowl to the table with the lettuce leaves. Spoon beef onto leaves, enclose, and enjoy.

NOTE *For a less spicy version, remove the seeds of the chilies. For an even milder dish, substitute ¼ cup minced red bell pepper.*

ELD

6 servings

serving (4)
ries 299, protein 22 g,
8 g, sodium 664 mg,
ohydrates 11 g,
ssium 350 mg

ME

to 25 minutes
preparation
8 minutes cooking

INGREDIENTS

1 pound medium shrimp
1 tablespoon cornstarch
3 cloves garlic
1 tablespoon salted black beans
3 tablespoons oil
6 slices gingerroot, 1/4 inch thick
1/4 pound ground pork or beef
3 scallions, in 1-inch pieces
1 medium egg, beaten

SAUCE A

1 tablespoon dry sherry
1 tablespoon thin soy sauce
1/2 teaspoon sugar

SAUCE B

1 1/4 tablespoons cornstarch
3/4 cup chicken broth

Peel the shrimp ①. Make a deep incision along the back; remove and discard the vein ②. Rinse thoroughly, pat dry, and coat with cornstarch. Peel and smash the garlic. Rinse the black beans under hot water, then drain well. In separate bowls, combine the sherry, soy sauce, and sugar and the cornstarch and chicken broth.

Cook the shrimp in boiling salted (1 teaspoon) water for 30 to 40 seconds. Drain and pat dry. Place on the work platter.

Heat a wok and add the oil. Heat for 15 seconds, then add the ginger slices. Stir until lightly browned, then add the garlic. Stir until lightly browned. Remove and discard both.

Add the salted beans, stir for 10 seconds, then add the ground pork. Stir vigorously to mix and break up the pork granules. Cook until the pork is no longer pink, then add the scallion pieces. Stir another 30 seconds, add the shrimp, and stir to mix well.

Mix Sauce A and pour down the sides of the wok, stirring all the while. Shovel the contents of the wok to one side. Mix Sauce B and pour down the vacated side of the wok. Stir to thicken with the point of the spatula. Mix with the shrimp ③.

Reduce the heat. Pour the beaten egg over the shrimp. Allow to set for 15 seconds, then fold in slowly until soft threads appear. Stir gently to mix. Remove to a platter and serve immediately.

ELD

o 6 servings

serving (4)
ries 407, protein 22 g,
30 g, sodium 840 mg,
ohydrates 14 g,
ssium 456 mg

ME

to 20 minutes
preparation
minutes chilling
o 6 minutes cooking

INGREDIENTS

I pound boneless pork loin
¼ teaspoon sugar
I tablespoon dry sherry
I small egg white
Cornstarch to coat
6–7 tablespoons oil
6 scallions
½ pound bean sprouts
4 cloves garlic
6 knobs gingerroot, I-inch wide
I teaspoon salt

SAUCE

⅔ cup chicken broth
2 teaspoons dry sherry
Salt to taste
White pepper to taste
I tablespoon cornstarch

Trim pork of top fat. Wrap and freeze until firm but not frozen, then cut across grain into ⅛-inch slices. Then cut with grain into thin shreds ①. Place in a bowl; add sugar and wine. Mix, add egg white, and mix again. Dust with cornstarch and mix again. Refrigerate at least 30 minutes. Bring to room temperature and coat with I tablespoon oil before cooking.

Wash and trim scallions. Cut greens into 2-inch pieces; cut root ends into quarters ②. Plunge sprouts into a large bowl of cold water and push under several times. Remove green husks as they float to the top, then drain sprouts and pat dry. Peel and lightly smash the garlic. Smash the ginger. Combine the sauce ingredients and mix well to dissolve the cornstarch.

Heat a wok. Add 3 tablespoons oil and heat for 15 to 20 seconds. Add ginger and swirl about. When ginger starts to brown, add garlic. Reduce heat and stir until garlic starts to brown. Remove and discard both.

Return heat to high. Add half the pork shreds and stir to coat with oil. Separate shreds, stirring constantly ③, then remove with strainer to a platter when pork is lightly browned. Cook remaining shreds and remove. Add more oil to wok if necessary. Stir in the salt, add the scallions, and stir 10 to 15 seconds. Add the sprouts. Stir 15 seconds, then remove contents of wok to work platter.

Add sauce to the wok. Stir to thicken and clarify. Add pork, sprouts, and scallions and stir to mix. Remove to serving platter. Serve immediately.

ELD

o 6 servings

serving (4)
ries 315, protein 28 g,
17 g, sodium 637 mg,
ohydrates 12 g,
ssium 422 mg

ME

minutes preparation
our pressing
to 30 minutes cooking

INGREDIENTS

2 pads fresh firm bean curd
12 dried black mushrooms
½ of a 3½-pound chicken
2 teaspoons cornstarch
1 piece gingerroot, 2 inches long

MARINADE

2 tablespoons dry sherry
1 tablespoon thin soy sauce
1 tablespoon oyster sauce
1 teaspoon sugar
1 tablespoon oriental sesame oil
Freshly ground pepper

Line a baking tray with a double layer of paper towels. Place the bean curd on the towels and cover with a double layer of more towels. Place another baking tray atop these towels and weight down with a heavy book. Press the bean curd in this manner for at least 1 hour. This process removes excess water and prevents diluting the final flavor.

Soak the mushrooms in hot water for 20 to 30 minutes.

Have the half-chicken cut into 16 pieces. Leave on the bone. Place the cornstarch in a large bowl and add the marinade. Mix well, then add the chicken to the bowl. Mix well to coat with marinade. Let stand for at least 15 minutes.

Peel the ginger; cut 8 to 10 thin slices across the grain. Squeeze the softened mushrooms dry, then remove and discard stems ①. Cut the mushrooms in half. Cut the pressed bean curd into 9 pieces each ②.

Place a 12-inch steaming rack in a steaming wok. Pour 6 cups of hot water into the wok, cover, and bring to the boil. Place the chicken pieces on a 10-inch plate, interspersing them with the mushrooms, ginger, and bean curd. Place the plate on the steaming rack ③, cover with the domed lid, and steam over high heat for 20 minutes. Remove the plate with a plate lifter. Place on another plate and serve immediately.

VARIATION If you wish more color, add 2 washed and trimmed scallions cut into 2-inch pieces. You may also top the finished dish with a tablespoon or so of oyster sauce.

YIELD

to 6 servings
serving (4)
ories 376, protein 22 g,
22 g, sodium 1332 mg,
oohydrates 26 g,
assium 615 mg

TIME

to 40 minutes
preparation
minutes cooking

INGREDIENTS

1 pound sea scallops
2 teaspoons dry sherry
2 teaspoons thin soy sauce
¼ teaspoon sugar
Cornstarch to coat
¼ pound snow peas
½ cup oil
6–8 dried chilies
Peel of ½ orange, broken into 1-inch
    pieces
6 pieces gingerroot, sliced ¼ inch thick

4–5 cloves garlic
3 scallions, white parts only

SAUCE

2 tablespoons thin soy sauce
2 tablespoons water
2 teaspoons oyster sauce
1 teaspoon oriental sesame oil
1 tablespoon sugar
1 teaspoon chili oil
2 teaspoons cornstarch mixed with 1
    tablespoon water (optional)

Cut scallops across the grain into ¼-inch discs ①. Add sherry, soy sauce, and sugar. Mix well. Sprinkle cornstarch on top and mix again. Reserve.

Place a colander in the sink. Bring 2 quarts water to the boil. Remove caps and side strings of snow peas, as well as bottom tip ②. Add peas to boiling water and stir until color changes to bright green (no longer than 10 seconds). Drain in the colander and douse immediately with cold water to stop the cooking. Dry with toweling and reserve.

Heat a wok and add the oil. Heat ½ minute, then add the chilies. Cook until the color changes to dark brown. Add the orange peel and ginger; when the ginger starts to brown, add the garlic and scallions. When the garlic browns, remove and discard the solids and strain the oil into a heatproof bowl. Wash and dry the wok.

Combine the sauce ingredients except for the cornstarch mixture.

Reheat the wok until smoking and add half the seasoned oil. Heat for 10 seconds, and add one-third the scallops. Stir over high heat and remove to a platter when the edges begin to brown lightly ③. Do the remaining scallops in 2 batches, adding just enough oil to keep the wok lubricated. Remove to the work platter.

Add 1 tablespoon oil to wok if needed. Add the snow peas and stir vigorously for 10 seconds, then add the scallops and stir to mix. Give the sauce a stir, then add down the sides of the wok. Stir to coat the scallops and peas. If the sauce is thin, trickle in half the cornstarch mixture and thicken with the tip of the spatula. Give a big stir to mix well. Remove to a platter and serve immediately.

YIELD

to 6 servings
serving (4)
ries 395, protein 13 g,
31 g, sodium 732 mg,
ohydrates 12 g,
ssium 665 mg

TIME

to 30 minutes
preparation
o 5 minutes cooking

INGREDIENTS

8 dried black mushrooms
I cup shredded Roast
  Pork (Recipe 32)
I small red pepper
I small green pepper
I large piece bamboo shoot
I large carrot
½ pound bean sprouts
4 scallions
I piece gingerroot, about 3 inches
Oil for stir-frying

SAUCE

2 tablespoons thin soy sauce
I tablespoon dry sherry
I tablespoon oriental sesame oil
2 teaspoons red wine vinegar
2 teaspoons sugar

Soak the mushrooms in hot water to soften. Cut the pork into 3-inch shreds. Core and seed the peppers ①, then shred. Cut 6 thin lengthwise slices from the bamboo shoot ②; shred the slices into matchstick-sized pieces. Cut a 3-inch piece from the large end of the carrot, then peel and cut into thin slices; cut the slices into matchstick shreds ③. Rinse the sprouts, and drain and dry well. Wash and trim the scallions, then split in half and cut into 3-inch pieces.

Drain the mushrooms, squeeze dry, and remove and discard the stems; shred the caps. Peel the ginger and cut 3 thin lengthwise slices then cut into thin shreds. Put all the shredded ingredients on a large platter. Combine the sauce ingredients.

Heat a wok. Add 3 tablespoons oil, heat for 15 seconds, then add the pork, mushrooms, and peppers. Stir for 30 seconds. Remove to the work platter with a strainer. Add 2 tablespoons oil, heat for 10 seconds, then add the ginger and carrot. Stir for 30 seconds, add the bamboo, stir another 30 seconds, and then add the bean sprouts and scallions. Put the pork back in, along with the peppers and mushrooms. Stir to mix well. Stir the sauce and pour down the sides of the wok. Mix well, remove to a platter, and serve immediately.

TIR-FRIED CORNUCOPIA

ELD

o 6 servings
' serving (4)
ries 179, protein 4 g,
12 g, sodium 403 mg,
oohydrates 17 g,
assium 579 mg

ME

to 25 minutes
preparation
o 4 minutes cooking

INGREDIENTS

3 stalks celery
1 small yellow onion
2 large red bell peppers
3 stalks bok choy
1 small zucchini
20 snow peas
3–4 tablespoons oil

SAUCE

1 tablespoon thin soy sauce
1/2 teaspoon wine or cider vinegar
1 teaspoon dry sherry
1/2 teaspoon sugar

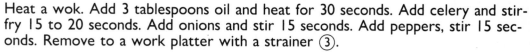

Wash, trim, and string celery. Peel onion, quarter, and separate into sections ①. Remove tops from peppers and discard seeds; cut peppers into 1½-inch strips. Trim the root end and most of the green leaves of the bok choy. Split the zucchini in half; set one half aside for another use. Cut the celery, peppers, bok choy, and zucchini on the bias into bite-sized pieces ②. Blanch the snow peas (see Recipe 18). Combine sauce ingredients.

Heat a wok. Add 3 tablespoons oil and heat for 30 seconds. Add celery and stir-fry 15 to 20 seconds. Add onions and stir 15 seconds. Add peppers, stir 15 seconds. Remove to a work platter with a strainer ③.

Add remaining oil if necessary and heat 10 seconds. Add bok choy and zucchini, and stir 15 seconds. Put the celery, onions, and peppers back in wok, then add the snow peas. Stir sauce, and pour down the sides of the wok. Stir to mix well, remove to a platter, and serve immediately.

VARIATION *Top with lightly toasted sesame seeds or top with 1 to 2 teaspoons oriental sesame oil.*

NOTE *Proportions given for vegetables are suggestions. You may feature or diminish the role of any as desired. The other half of the zucchini may be used for Recipe 9.*

YELD

o 6 servings
r serving (4)
ries 579, protein 21 g,
49 g, sodium 1066 mg,
ohydrates 13 g,
assium 265 mg

IME

to 18 minutes
preparation
our cooking

INGREDIENTS

1 small rack spareribs
3 tablespoons cornstarch
5 cloves garlic
1 knob gingerroot about 2 inches long
1 tablespoon salted black beans
2 scallions
1/2–1 teaspoon red pepper flakes
1/4 cup oil
3 tablespoons thin soy sauce

1 tablespoon red wine vinegar
2 teaspoons dry sherry
2 teaspoons sugar

Have the butcher cut the ribs across the bone into 1-inch strips. Cut the ribs into individual pieces between the bones ①, place in a bowl, and coat with the cornstarch.

Peel and mince the garlic. Peel the ginger, cut 5 very thin lengthwise slices, then cut these into thin shreds. Cut the shreds into fine mince ②. Rinse the beans under hot water. Dice the scallions into 1/4-inch pieces. Combine the garlic, beans, scallions, and chili flakes. In another bowl, combine the sauce ingredients.

Place a 12-inch bamboo steamer in your steaming wok. Add sufficient water to touch the bottom of the steamer basket, cover with the steamer top, and bring to the boil.

Heat your oil-cooking wok. Add the oil and heat for 1 minute. Add the ribs and stir vigorously to coat with oil; toss for 2 minutes. Make a well in the center of the wok. Add the dry ingredients and stir for 15 seconds with the point of the spatula, then toss to coat the ribs.

Re-stir the sauce to mix the sugar. Pour around the sides of the wok, then stir to coat the ribs ③. Toss vigorously for 15 seconds. Remove to a plate.

Lower the plate of ribs into the bamboo steamer. Cover and steam the ribs over high heat for 45 minutes. Add hot water to the wok from time to time to replenish that lost through steaming. After 45 minutes, remove the ribs with a plate lifter or bring the plate and the steamer basket to the table.

YIELD

to 6 servings
r serving (4)
ith Sauce A)

ories 610, protein 19 g,
40 g, sodium 1455 mg,
bohydrates 42 g,
tassium 354 mg

TIME

minutes preparation
to 15 minutes cooking

INGREDIENTS

1 pound medium shrimp in their shells
½ head iceberg lettuce
8 cups oil

BATTER

1½ cups all-purpose flour
1 tablespoon baking powder
1 teaspoon salt
½ cup oil
1–1¼ cups cold water

SAUCE A

1½ tablespoons thin soy sauce
3 tablespoons mild vinegar
2 tablespoons shredded gingerroot
1 tablespoon oriental sesame oil

SAUCE B

2 tablespoons hoisin sauce
1 tablespoon tomato catsup
1 teaspoon chili sauce (Red Devil or
   the like)
1 teaspoon dry sherry
1 tablespoon minced scallion

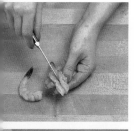

Remove the shells from the shrimp but leave the last segment and the tails. Split the shrimp down the back until almost completely open ①. Remove the vein. Place the shrimp in a bowl of ice water.

Combine the dry ingredients for the batter. Mix well, then add the oil a little at a time until oil and flour are thoroughly mixed; break up any large lumps. Now add the water a little at a time ②, stirring constantly in one direction. Eventually, the batter will become smooth and silky. Stop adding water when you attain the consistency of a thin pancake batter. Allow the batter to rest, covered, for at least 15 minutes.

Prepare sauce A, B, or both. Shred the lettuce and place on a platter. Cover with clear wrap until ready for use.

Place the oil in a wok and heat to 375 degrees. While the oil is heating, drain the shrimp, pat dry, and dip in the batter, leaving the tails exposed for easy handling. Line a work platter with paper toweling.

Place 8 to 10 shrimp in the hot oil and cook until the batter turns a golden brown. Remove with a large strainer to the work platter ③. Do the remaining shrimp in the same manner, making sure that the oil reaches 375 degrees before adding the shrimp.

Remove the covering from the lettuce. Place the sauce bowl(s) in the center. Place the shrimp, tails up, around the perimeter of the platter. Serve immediately.

VARIATION For additional color, garnish with lemon and tomato wedges.

23

YIELD

to 6 servings

r serving (4)
ories 401, protein 23 g,
19 g, sodium 1238 mg,
bohydrates 36 g,
assium 601 mg

TIME

to 15 minutes
preparation
minutes marinating
to 20 minutes cooking

INGREDIENTS

¼ cup dry sherry
2 tablespoons soy sauce
I pound any firm-fleshed fish fillet
4–5 fresh chilies, preferably red
3 scallions
I knob fresh gingerroot, about 3
   inches
6 cloves garlic
½ cup water
½ cup tomato catsup
¼ cup red wine vinegar

2 tablespoons Red Devil or your
   favorite chili sauce
8 cups oil
½ cup cornstarch, approximately
2 tablespoons cornstarch mixed with
   4 tablespoons cold water

Combine the sherry and soy sauce in a bowl. Lightly score the fillets both sides ①. Marinate in soy sauce mixture for 30 minutes.

Open the chilies lengthwise ②, then remove and discard the seeds; cut into thin strips, then into small dice. Peel the ginger and cut 8 thin lengthwise slices. Shred and then mince the ginger. Peel, smash and mince garlic. Wash and trim scallions, split in half, then cut into ⅛-inch dice. Combine minced ingredients in a bowl. Combine water, catsup, vinegar, and Red Devil sauce in another bowl.

Place 8 cups oil in a wok and heat to 375 degrees. At the same time, remove ¼ cup oil to a heavy skillet, heat, and add the minced ingredients. Stir for I minute, add the liquid mixture, bring to the boil, reduce to a bare simmer, and cover.

Drain the fish fillets. Pat dry and dredge in cornstarch. When the oil reaches 375 degrees, shake off the excess starch, lower the fillets into the oil ③, and fry until lightly browned. Remove with the large strainer. Allow the oil to heat for 2 minutes, then return the fillets to the oil for 15 seconds to further crisp the outside. Remove to a platter.

Remove cover from the skillet. Re-stir the cornstarch and water, then slowly trickle into the sauce. Stir constantly until the desired consistency is reached. (Some like it thin.) Pour sauce over fillets and serve immediately.

NOTE This sauce may be used over Steamed Whole Fish, in which case omit all seasonings but the wine, or use it over the Deep-fried Crispy Shrimp. (See Recipes 4 or 22.)

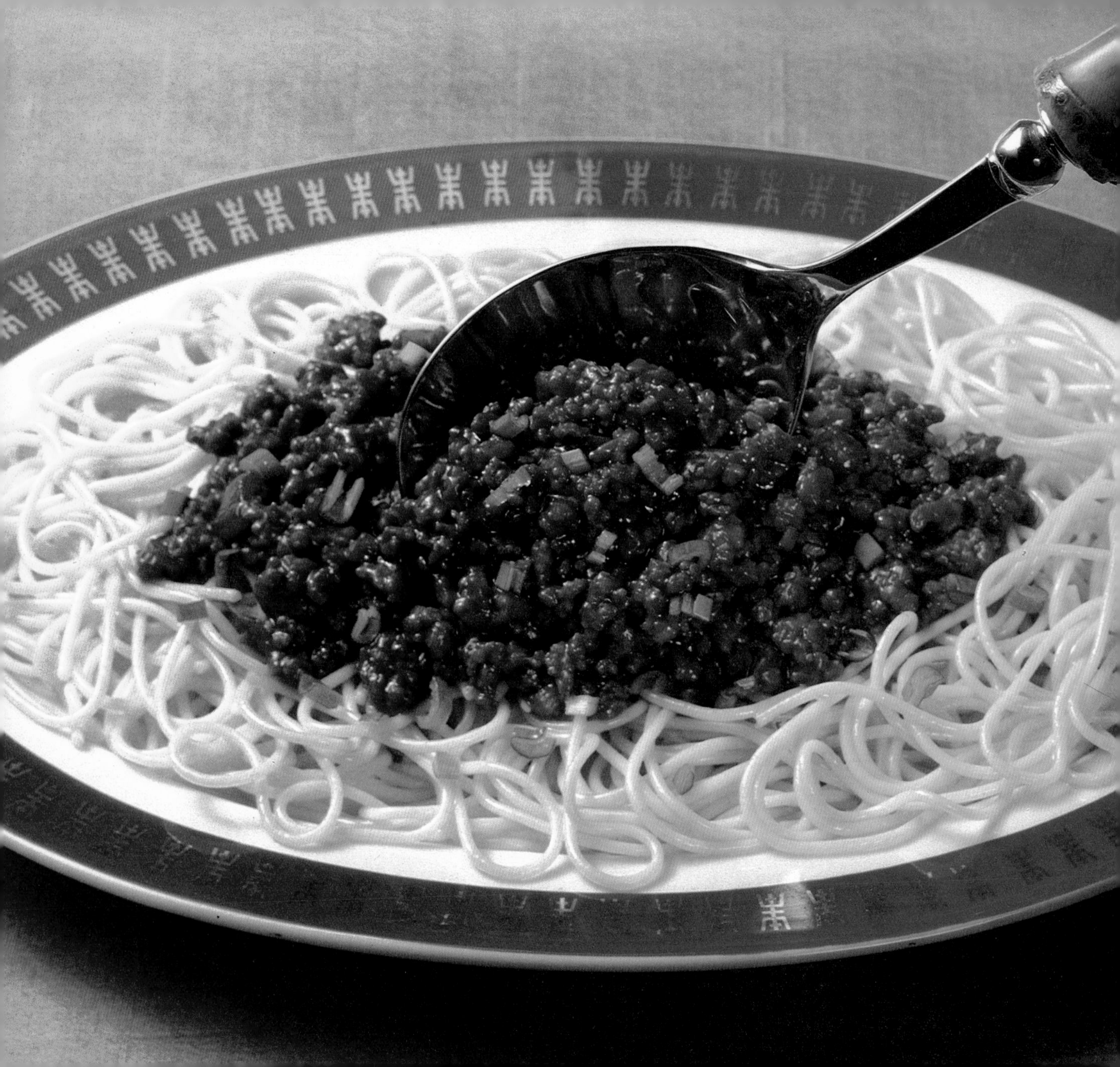

‎ELD

‎o 6 servings

‎ serving (4)
‎ries 950, protein 35 g,
‎41 g, sodium 2095 mg,
‎ohydrates 109 g,
‎assium 606 mg

‎ME

‎ to 35 minutes
‎preparation
‎ to 25 minutes cooking

INGREDIENTS

4 cloves garlic
1 teaspoon dry sherry
1 large onion
1 pound ground pork or beef
3 tablespoons oil
1 pound vermicelli
2 tablespoons cornstarch
5 tablespoons chicken broth
2 tablespoons oriental sesame oil
½ cup diced scallion greens for
   garnish

SAUCE

¼ cup hoisin sauce
¼ cup black soy sauce
¼ cup chicken broth
¼ cup dry sherry
2 tablespoons sugar

Peel, smash, and mince the garlic ①. Moisten with dry sherry. Dice the onion to yield 1½ cups ②. Break up the ground meat with a knife to facilitate cooking. Combine the sauce ingredients.

Bring a large kettle of water to the boil. Heat a wok and add the oil. Heat for 10 seconds, then add the garlic. Stir for 10 to 15 seconds but avoid browning. Add the diced onion and stir until the onion begins to wilt. Add the ground meat and stir vigorously to separate the grains. When the meat has lost its raw color, add the sauce. Stir to mix well ③, cover, and let the sauce simmer for 10 minutes or longer.

Add a tablespoon each of salt and oil to the boiling water, add the noodles, and cook to the *al dente* stage. Drain, rinse, and place in a large bowl.

Combine the cornstarch and chicken broth. Slowly pour into the wok, thicken the sauce to the desired consistency and pour over the noodles. Top with sesame oil and serve immediately, garnished with the scallion greens.

NOTE *If you have access to a Chinese market, substitute sweet bean sauce for the hoisin sauce. If you have the time, press bean curd (see Recipe 17) until very firm, cut into small dice, and add to the sauce just before serving.*

YIELD

6 servings
serving (4)
ries 653, protein 20 g,
37 g, sodium 1218 mg,
oohydrates 60 g,
assium 455 mg

TIME

to 25 minutes
preparation
to 15 minutes cooking

INGREDIENTS

8 ounces rice vermicelli
3 large eggs
Salt and pepper
1 yellow onion
10 snow peas
1 red bell pepper, about 3 inches high
2 cups bean sprouts
6–7 tablespoons oil
1 cup shredded Roast Pork
 (Recipe 32)

SAUCE

½ cup chicken broth
1½ tablespoons thin soy sauce
1 tablespoon black soy sauce
1 tablespoon hoisin sauce

Put the noodles in a bowl. Cover with tepid water and soak until softened, about 15 to 20 minutes ①. Beat the eggs; add salt and pepper to taste. Peel and shred the onion. String the snow peas, then shred each into 4 pieces. Cut the pepper into ⅛-inch lengthwise strips. Plunge the bean sprouts into a bowl of cold water and push under several times; remove green husks as they float to the top, then drain and dry. Drain the noodles; shake well to remove excess water. Mix the sauce ingredients.

Heat a heavy (preferably cast-iron) skillet. Add the oil and heat for 30 seconds, then drain the oil into a heatproof bowl but leave the pan slick. Add one-third of the egg and swirl to coat the entire bottom, forming a thin crêpe ②. When firm, remove with a spatula. Add more oil if necessary and make 2 more crêpes. Allow to cool. Cut in half, then into shreds.

Heat a wok. Add 2 tablespoons oil and heat 15 seconds. Add the pork, onion, and pepper. Stir until the onion becomes translucent, then remove solids to a work platter. Add 2 more tablespoons oil and heat 5 seconds. Add the snow peas and bean sprouts. Stir for 15 to 20 seconds, then put pork and other ingredients back in. Stir to mix, add the shredded egg and the noodles, and mix again ③. Pour the sauce down the sides of the wok. Stir and toss lightly to coat everything evenly, and remove to a serving platter. Serve immediately.

VARIATION *Any cooked shredded meat can be used or, if you prefer, omit the meat.*

26

ELD

o 6 servings
r serving (4)
ries 500, protein 38 g,
32 g, sodium 957 mg,
bohydrates 13 g,
assium 489 mg

IME

minutes preparation
minutes marinating
minutes cooking

INGREDIENTS

1½ pounds flank steak, trimmed, 3 to
   3½ inches wide
2 teaspoons thin soy sauce
2 teaspoons dry sherry
1 egg white
Cornstarch to coat
1 cup plus 1 tablespoon oil
2 fat leeks about 1½ inches in
   diameter
1 large piece bamboo shoot

SAUCE

¼ cup hoisin sauce
1 tablespoon dry sherry
1 teaspoon black soy sauce
2 tablespoons oriental sesame oil

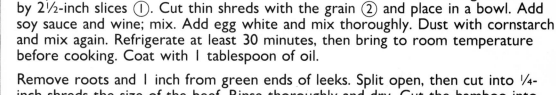

Wrap beef and chill until firm, not frozen. Cut on the bias across the grain into ¼ by 2½-inch slices ①. Cut thin shreds with the grain ② and place in a bowl. Add soy sauce and wine; mix. Add egg white and mix thoroughly. Dust with cornstarch and mix again. Refrigerate at least 30 minutes, then bring to room temperature before cooking. Coat with 1 tablespoon of oil.

Remove roots and 1 inch from green ends of leeks. Split open, then cut into ¼-inch shreds the size of the beef. Rinse thoroughly and dry. Cut the bamboo into ⅛-inch slices, then into ⅛-inch shreds also the size of the beef ③. Combine the sauce ingredients.

Heat the remaining oil in a wok to 300 degrees. Add half the beef, stir to separate, and cook until the beef changes color. Remove with a large strainer to a work platter. Reheat the oil and add the remaining beef. Remove meat to the platter; drain the oil into a heatproof bowl.

Add 3 tablespoons of the oil to the wok. Heat for 30 seconds, then add the shredded bamboo. Stir for 30 seconds, then add the leeks. Cook until leeks begin to wilt. Remove bamboo and leeks with a strainer to a separate platter.

Add another tablespoon of oil to the wok. Add sauce and bring to the bubble. Add beef; stir to coat. Remove to a serving platter; top with the leeks and bamboo and serve immediately.

27

ELD

6 servings
serving (4)
ies 353, protein 27 g,
0 g, sodium 1058 mg,
ohydrates 18 g,
ssium 688 mg

ME

to 25 minutes
reparation
6 minutes cooking

INGREDIENTS

1 pound chicken livers
Cornstarch to coat
3 knobs gingerroot, 1 inch long
2 scallions
1 small head cauliflower
1 teaspoon salt
1 large red bell pepper
4–5 tablespoons oil

SAUCE

2 tablespoons oyster sauce
2 teaspoons A-1 Sauce
2 teaspoons dry sherry
Ground pepper

Trim the livers of fat and membranes ①. Discard mealy pieces. Place livers in a bowl, coat with cornstarch, and mix. Smash the ginger. Wash, trim, and cut scallions into 1-inch pieces.

Break the cauliflower heads into uniform bite-sized pieces ②. Bring 2 quarts water to the boil, add 1 teaspoon salt, and blanch the cauliflower for 45 seconds. Drain, cool, and dry.

Cut the red pepper into 1-inch squares. Combine the sauce ingredients.

Heat a wok. Add 3 tablespoons oil, heat for 30 seconds, then add ginger. Stir and cook until browned; discard. Add half the livers. Stir until browned and lightly spongy when pressed with the spatula. Remove to a work platter. Cook the remaining livers, adding oil down the sides ③ of wok if necessary. Remove.

Add the scallions and peppers; stir 30 seconds. Add the cauliflower and livers; stir 15 seconds. Pour the sauce down the sides of the wok, stirring to coat thoroughly. Remove to a platter and serve immediately.

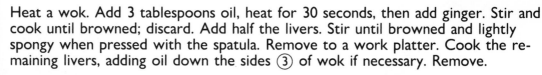